THE ULTIMATE

Turtles

BOOK

Imprint: Bellanova Books
ISBN: 978-619-264-169-6

Contents

Introduction

Get ready for an exciting journey as we dive into the amazing world of turtles! These lovely creatures have been around for millions of years, and they come in all shapes and sizes. We'll look at what makes turtles so unique and introduce you to the three main types of turtles: **sea turtles, freshwater turtles,** and **tortoises.** Did you know there were different types?!

WHAT MAKES A TURTLE A TURTLE?

Turtles are reptiles, which means they're cold-blooded and have scaly skin. But what sets them apart from other reptiles like snakes and lizards?

Here are a few things that make a turtle a turtle:

SHELLS Turtles are famous for their hard, protective shells. A turtle's shell is made up of two parts: the top part (called the carapace) and the bottom part (called the plastron). The shell is actually part of their skeleton and is fused to their spine and ribcage!

Fun Fact: Did you know that a turtle's shell grows with them throughout their life?

NO TEETH Turtles don't have teeth! Instead, they have sharp beaks that they use to bite and tear their food.

SLOW AND STEADY Turtles are known for their slow movement on land, but some species can be quite fast in water! The saying "slow and steady wins the race" comes from the classic fable about the tortoise and the hare.

THE THREE TYPES OF TURTLES

Now that we know what makes a turtle a turtle, let's meet the three main types of these fascinating creatures:

SEA TURTLES

Sea turtles are turtles that live in the ocean and are specially adapted for life in the water. They have large, paddle-like flippers to help them swim and can hold their breath for a long time.

EXAMPLES: Green sea turtle, loggerhead sea turtle, and leatherback sea turtle.

FRESHWATER TURTLES

Freshwater turtles live in lakes, rivers, and ponds. They have webbed feet to help them swim and are often seen basking in the sun on rocks or logs.

EXAMPLES: Painted turtle, red-eared slider, and snapping turtle.

TORTOISES

Tortoises are land-dwelling turtles with thick, sturdy legs made for walking on solid ground. They typically have a large, dome-shaped shell and eat plants.

EXAMPLES: Galapagos giant tortoise, sulcata tortoise, and Russian tortoise.

Fun Fact: All tortoises are turtles, but not all turtles are tortoises.

So now you know the different types of turtles, let's explore more about these wonderful shelled creatures, their habitats, and their unique characteristics.

THE WORLD OF TURTLES

From tropical beaches to dense forests and even arid deserts, turtles have found their way to nearly every corner of the world. These amazing creatures have adapted to all kinds of environments. Let's take a journey around the globe and explore the diverse habitats where turtles call home.

Sea turtles are the world travelers of the turtle family. They spend most of their lives swimming through the vast oceans, traveling thousands of miles in search of food and nesting sites.

Tropical and subtropical beaches: Sea turtles lay their eggs on sandy shores, usually in warm, tropical or subtropical regions.

Coral reefs: These colorful underwater gardens are a favorite feeding ground for some sea turtles, like the green sea turtle. They graze on the seagrass and algae that grow among the coral.

Open ocean: The largest sea turtle, the leatherback, prefers the open ocean and can be found roaming the seas at depths of over 3,000 feet (914 m)!

RIVERS, LAKES, AND WETLANDS

Freshwater turtles are found in a range of watery habitats, from slow-moving rivers to crystal-clear lakes. They're great swimmers and can often be seen basking in the sun on rocks or logs. Some freshwater turtle habitats include:

RIVERS AND STREAMS

Many freshwater turtles, like the North American snapping turtle, inhabit rivers and streams with plenty of hiding spots among rocks and underwater vegetation.

LAKES AND PONDS The red-eared slider and painted turtle are commonly seen in lakes and ponds, where they can easily find their favorite foods like aquatic plants, insects, and small fish.

WETLANDS AND MARSHES Some turtles, like the diamondback terrapin, make their homes in wetlands and marshes, thriving in the brackish water where fresh and saltwater mix.

SLOW AND STEADY ON LAND

Unlike their aquatic cousins, tortoises are land-dwelling turtles that can be found in a range of terrestrial habitats. They may move slowly on their sturdy legs, but they're expert survivors in some of the harshest environments. Let's check out a few places where tortoises live:

FORESTS: Some tortoises, like the yellow-footed tortoise, live in the humid rainforests of South America, where they feast on fallen fruit and leaves.

GRASSLANDS: The African spurred tortoise, also known as the sulcata tortoise, roams the grasslands and savannas of Africa, grazing on grasses and other plants.

DESERTS: The desert tortoise is a true survivor, living in the harsh deserts of the southwestern United States and Mexico. They're specially adapted to withstand extreme heat and can go long periods without water.

ISLANDS: The famous Galapagos giant tortoises are found only on the Galapagos Islands, where they've evolved into unique subspecies, each adapted to the specific conditions of their island home.

As we've seen, turtles have conquered all kinds of environments on our planet! Their incredible adaptability is one of the reasons they've been around for millions of years. So next time you're near a beach, a lake, or even a desert, keep an eye out for our shelled friends, because they might be closer than you think!

THE ULTIMATE BOOK

MEET THE SPECIES

In this chapter, we'll introduce you to some of the most iconic and fascinating turtle species from around the world. From the leatherback sea turtle, the largest of all living turtles, to the tiny speckled padloper tortoise, the smallest turtle species in the world, we'll explore a diverse range of species that are adapted to thrive in a variety of habitats.

There are over 350 species of turtles in the world, and while we won't be able to cover them all, we'll showcase a selection of species that are representative of the diversity and wonder of these amazing animals.

Meet the green sea turtle, a gentle giant that plays a crucial role in maintaining healthy coral reefs.

Fact file

HABITAT	Tropical and subtropical oceans
SIZE	Up to 5 feet (1.5 m) long and 700 pounds (317 kg)
SPECIAL FEATURES	Named for the greenish color of their fat, these herbivores feast on seagrass and algae.
FUN FACT	Green sea turtles can hold their breath for several hours while resting underwater!

LOGGERHEAD SEA TURTLE (*Caretta caretta*)

The loggerhead sea turtle is the largest of the hard-shelled sea turtles. It is a strong-jawed turtle that is known for its incredible long-distance navigation skills.

Image: Matt Kieffer

<h1 style="text-align:center">Fact file</h1>

HABITAT	Coastal waters and open oceans around the world
SIZE	Up to 3.5 feet (1 m) long and 400 pounds (181 kg)
SPECIAL FEATURES	Loggerheads have strong, muscular jaws that allow them to crush hard-shelled prey like crabs and sea urchins.
FUN FACT	Loggerhead sea turtles have an incredible sense of direction and can navigate thousands of miles back to the beach where they were born to lay their eggs.

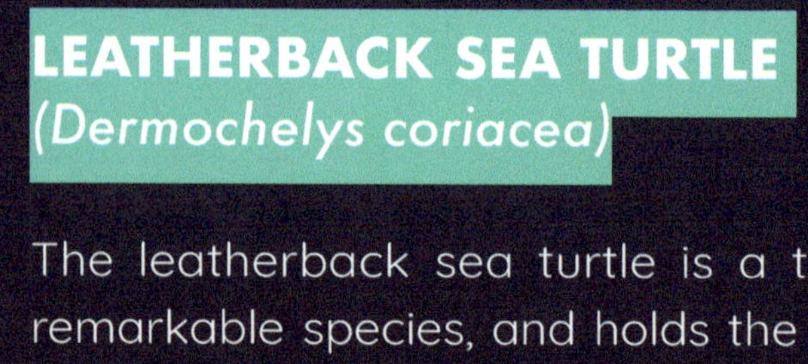

LEATHERBACK SEA TURTLE
(Dermochelys coriacea)

The leatherback sea turtle is a truly remarkable species, and holds the title of being the largest turtle species in the world. Leatherback turtles also have unique adaptations that allow them to dive deeper than any other turtle species, with the ability to reach depths of over 4,000 feet (1,219 m) while searching for their favorite prey, jellyfish.

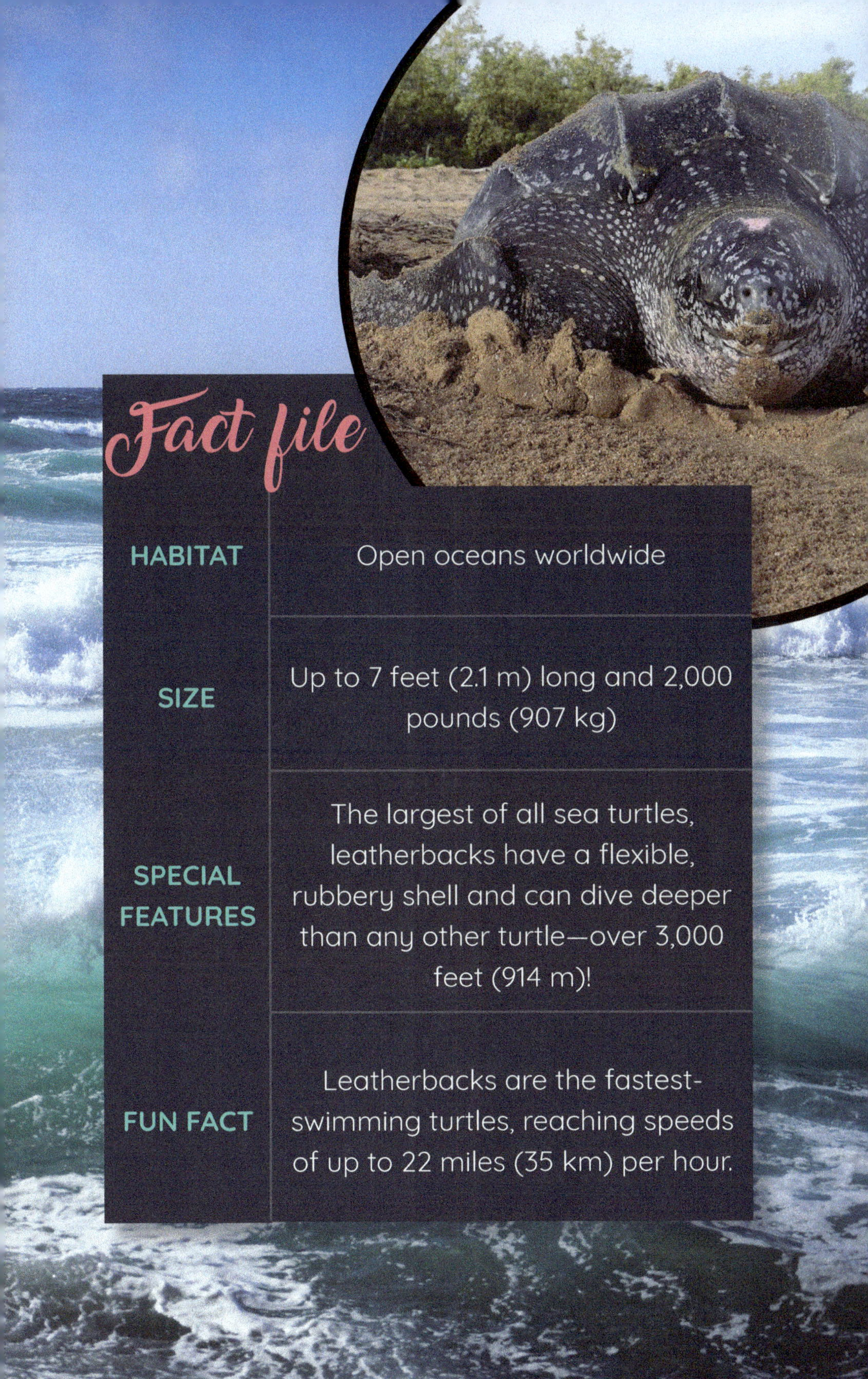

Fact file

HABITAT	Open oceans worldwide
SIZE	Up to 7 feet (2.1 m) long and 2,000 pounds (907 kg)
SPECIAL FEATURES	The largest of all sea turtles, leatherbacks have a flexible, rubbery shell and can dive deeper than any other turtle—over 3,000 feet (914 m)!
FUN FACT	Leatherbacks are the fastest-swimming turtles, reaching speeds of up to 22 miles (35 km) per hour.

Fact file

HABITAT	Freshwater habitats in North America
SIZE	Up to 10 inches (25 cm) long and about 0.5 to 1.5 pounds (0.2 to 0.7 kg)
SPECIAL FEATURES	These colorful turtles have intricate patterns on their shells, heads, and limbs that resemble paintings.
FUN FACT	These turtles are known for their resilience, as they can survive in a variety of different habitats, from wetlands to urban ponds, making them one of the most widespread turtle species in North America.

The painted turtle is a colorful species of freshwater turtle, known for its distinctive red and yellow stripes on its head and neck, and its smooth olive or black carapace. Painted turtles are excellent baskers, often seen sunning themselves on logs or rocks, and are commonly found in ponds, lakes, and other slow-moving bodies of water throughout North America.

RED-EARED SLIDER (*Trachemys scripta elegans*)

The red-eared slider is a popular pet turtle species that is native to the southern United States and northern Mexico. They are named for the red stripe on either side of their heads, which is often accompanied by a yellow stripe. Red-eared sliders are semi-aquatic, meaning they spend time both in the water and on land.

Fact file

HABITAT	Freshwater habitats in North America
SIZE	Up to 12 inches (30 cm) long
SPECIAL FEATURES	They are named for the red stripe on either side of their heads, which is often accompanied by a yellow stripe.
FUN FACT	Red-eared sliders can live up to 30 years in the wild and even longer in captivity!

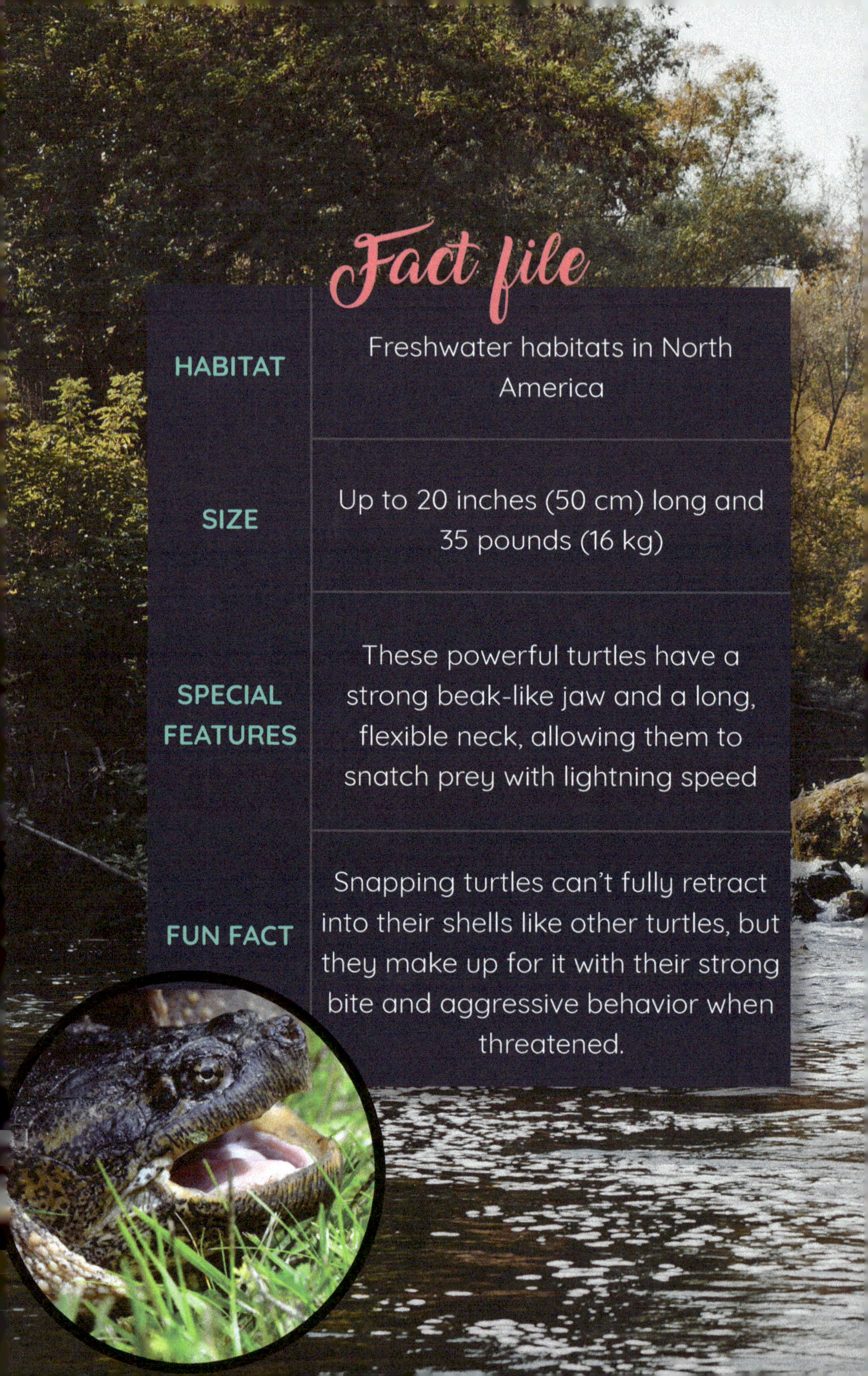

Fact file

HABITAT	Freshwater habitats in North America
SIZE	Up to 20 inches (50 cm) long and 35 pounds (16 kg)
SPECIAL FEATURES	These powerful turtles have a strong beak-like jaw and a long, flexible neck, allowing them to snatch prey with lightning speed
FUN FACT	Snapping turtles can't fully retract into their shells like other turtles, but they make up for it with their strong bite and aggressive behavior when threatened.

SNAPPING TURTLE (Chelydra serpentina)

The snapping turtle is a large freshwater turtle species found in North America. They are known for their powerful, beak-like jaws and lightning-fast bite, which they use to catch prey and defend themselves.

GALAPAGOS GIANT TORTOISE
(Chelonoidis spp.)

Say hello to the Galapagos giant tortoise, the largest living tortoise and a true symbol of the Galapagos Islands. The Galapagos giant tortoise is endemic to the Galapagos Islands, a volcanic archipelago off the coast of Ecuador in the Pacific Ocean. Unfortunately, the Galapagos giant tortoise was once on the brink of extinction due to hunting by humans and habitat loss, but conservation efforts have helped to increase their population in recent years.

HABITAT	Galapagos Islands
SIZE	Up to 5 feet (1.5 m) long and 550 pounds (250 kg)
SPECIAL FEATURES	The largest living tortoises, Galapagos giants are known for their massive, dome-shaped shells and slow, lumbering movements.
FUN FACT	These tortoises can live for over 100 years, making them one of the longest-lived vertebrates on Earth!

Fact file

HABITAT	Grasslands and savannas of Africa
SIZE	Up to 2.5 feet (0.76 m) long and 200 pounds (90 kg)
SPECIAL FEATURES	Also known as the African spurred tortoise, sulcatas have thick, sturdy legs and large, bony scales on their front legs for protection
FUN FACT	Sulcata tortoises dig burrows up to 30 feet (9 m) long in the wild to escape the extreme heat and stay cool!

Meet the sulcata tortoise, a fascinating reptile that is the third largest tortoise species in the world! These tortoises are native to the arid savannas of Africa and have a tough, spiky exterior that can help protect them from predators.

TURTLE LIFECYCLE

FROM HATCHLING TO ADULT

In this chapter, we'll explore the fascinating life cycle of turtles, from the moment they hatch to their adventures as adults. We'll learn about the various stages of their lives and the challenges they face along the way.

HATCHING

Turtle life begins in an egg, usually buried in a nest on a sandy beach or in the soil, depending on the species. After the mother has carefully laid her eggs and concealed the nest, she leaves her offspring to face the world on their own. The incubation period varies between species, but typically lasts between 45 to 70 days.

A female turtle laying her eggs.

When the time is right, the hatchlings use a special temporary tooth called the "**egg tooth**" to break open their shells. Once free, they must quickly make their way to the surface. For many turtles, this is a race against time as they must avoid predators such as birds, crabs, and raccoons that are eager to snatch them up.

FINDING THEIR WAY: THE JOURNEY TO THE WATER

After breaking free from their nest, the hatchlings must embark on the most perilous journey of their lives: reaching the water. For sea turtles, this means navigating their way to the ocean, while freshwater turtles and tortoises need to find a nearby pond, lake, or river. To find their way, turtles use a variety of cues such as the slope of the terrain, the sound of the waves, or even the Earth's magnetic field.

GROWING UP: THE JUVENILE YEARS

Once they've reached the water, the hatchlings face a whole new set of challenges. They must learn to find food, avoid predators, and navigate their new environment. As they grow, they will shed their outer layer of skin and develop new, larger scutes on their shells.

During this time, juvenile turtles are incredibly vulnerable, with many species experiencing a high mortality rate.

ADULTHOOD: SEARCHING FOR A MATE

As turtles reach adulthood, their focus shifts towards finding a mate and reproducing. Turtles use a variety of ways to attract mates, such as colorful displays, fancy dances, and gentle nuzzling. Once a suitable partner has been found, the turtles will mate, and the female will begin searching for the perfect spot to lay her eggs.

Adult turtles will continue to reproduce throughout their lives, laying multiple clutches of eggs each year in some species. This makes sure that there are always new generations of turtles to carry on their legacy. As they get older, turtles will face new challenges, such as changes in their environment, competition for resources, and the threat of predators.

However, turtles are an incredibly strong group of animals, and many species can live for several decades, or even over a century, in the wild!

TURTLE ANATOMY

In this chapter, we'll dive deep into the fascinating anatomy of turtles, learning about their unique body structures and the adaptations that help them survive. From their famous shells to their strong limbs and even their curious internal organs, let's find out what makes a turtle a turtle!

A turtle's most iconic feature is its shell! The shell is made up of two main parts: the carapace (the top part) and the plastron (the bottom part). These two parts are connected by a bridge on each side of the turtle's body. The shell is made up of a series of interlocking plates called scutes, which are made of keratin, the same material that makes up our hair and nails.

Turtle shells come in various shapes and sizes, depending on the species and their habitat. Some turtles have a streamlined, flat shell that helps them glide through the water with ease, while others have a more domed shape, perfect for protection on land.

THE HEAD, NECK, AND BEAK: SENSING AND EATING

Turtles have relatively small heads compared to their body size, but it's packed with sensory organs, such as eyes, ears, and nostrils. Their eyes have a protective layer called the **nictitating membrane** that helps keep them moist and clear of debris. Turtles have excellent vision and can see a wide range of colors.

Instead of teeth, turtles have a sharp, beak-like structure called the **tomium**. The shape and size of a turtle's beak can give you clues about its diet. Herbivorous turtles have broad, flat beaks for crushing and grinding plant material, while carnivorous turtles have more hooked beaks for capturing and tearing apart their prey.

Many turtles have a long, flexible neck that allows them to reach out and grab food or pull their head into their shell for protection.

WALKING, SWIMMING, AND DIGGING

Turtle limbs are specially adapted for their specific environment and lifestyle. Aquatic turtles have webbed feet or flippers, which help them to swim efficiently and maneuver through the water. Some sea turtles, such as the leatherback, have powerful front flippers that can propel them through the ocean at impressive speeds.

Land-dwelling turtles, like tortoises, have sturdy, columnar legs that support their weight and help them move across uneven terrain. Many tortoises also have sharp claws for digging burrows or scraping away soil to find food.

INTERNAL ORGANS: WHAT'S HIDING INSIDE

Inside their shells, turtles have a set of organs that help them survive and thrive. They have a three-chambered heart that pumps blood throughout their body, and their lungs are adapted for efficient gas exchange, allowing them to hold their breath for long periods while underwater.

Turtles have a unique feature called the **cloaca**, which serves as a single opening for their digestive, urinary, and reproductive systems. This multipurpose opening helps to conserve water and makes it easier for turtles to keep their internal organs protected within their shells.

MATE BOOK

Amazing
Adaptations

In this chapter, we'll look at some of the most incredible adaptations that turtles have developed to survive and thrive in various environments. From their impressive breathing techniques to their remarkable navigation skills, we'll discover the unique and turtley amazing abilities of these fascinating creatures.

So, let's shell out some knowledge and dive in!

How Turtles Survive Underwater

While all turtles need to breathe air, many aquatic species have developed some extraordinary ways to stay underwater for long periods. Some turtles can take small amounts of oxygen from water through their skin, particularly around their throat and the skin folds near their rear end. This process, known as **cutaneous respiration**, allows them to absorb just enough oxygen to survive while they're underwater!

Other turtles, such as the painted turtle, can lower their metabolism and enter a state of brumation, which is similar to hibernation, during cold months. This hugely reduces their oxygen needs and allows them to survive without breathing for several months!

Home on the Move:
The Multi-Purpose Shell

A turtle's shell is more than just a protective shield; it's also a mobile home and a multifunctional tool. The shell helps maintain body temperature by absorbing heat from the sun or providing insulation in colder environments. It also acts as a natural buoyancy aid, helping turtles to float and maintain their balance in the water.

In addition to protection, the shell serves as an anchor point for the turtle's muscles, allowing them to move their limbs, head, and tail effectively. Some turtle species, like the box turtle, can even close their shells completely, creating an impenetrable fortress against predators!

MAGNETIC NAVIGATION: THE TURTLE'S BUILT-IN GPS

Many turtle species, especially sea turtles, have an incredible ability to navigate vast distances across the ocean. They can find their way back to the exact beach where they were born to lay their eggs, sometimes traveling thousands of miles. But how do they do it?

Research suggests that turtles use the Earth's magnetic field to navigate, similar to a built-in GPS. They can detect subtle differences in the magnetic field and use this information to determine their position and direction. This amazing sense of direction helps them find their way back to their nesting grounds, even after years of being away.

Blending In with the Environment

Many turtle species have developed impressive camouflage and mimicry techniques to avoid predators and blend in with their surroundings. Some aquatic turtles, like the red-eared slider, have patterns on their shells that resemble the dappled sunlight on the water's surface, making them difficult to spot from above.

Land-dwelling turtles, like the desert tortoise, have colors and patterns that blend in seamlessly with their arid environment, allowing them to hide from predators in plain sight. Some turtles even have algae growing on their shells, providing them with a living layer of camouflage!

THE SECRETS OF TURTLE AGING

Turtles are among the longest-lived animals on Earth, with some species, like the Galapagos giant tortoise, living for over a century. So, what's the secret to their remarkable longevity?

One factor is their slow metabolism, which helps them conserve energy and reduces the wear and tear on their bodies. Some turtles also have an ability to repair damaged DNA, which can help to prevent age-related diseases and keep them healthy for longer periods.

THE ART OF COMMUNICATION: TURTLE TALK

Turtles may not be as vocal as birds or mammals, but they still have unique ways to communicate with each other. They rely on visual cues, body language, and even some sounds to convey messages to their fellow turtles.

For example, male turtles often use elaborate displays or gentle touches to court females, while some species, like the red-eared slider, have been known to produce low-frequency sounds underwater to communicate with each other. Understanding these subtle signals can be essential for turtles to find mates, establish territories, and avoid conflict.

Hibernation and Estivation: Surviving Extreme Conditions

Turtles have developed various strategies to survive in harsh or extreme conditions, such as hibernation and estivation. Hibernation is a period of inactivity and reduced metabolism that allows turtles to survive cold winter months when food is scarce. Many freshwater turtles hibernate by burying themselves in the mud at the bottom of a pond or river, where they can remain dormant for months.

Estivation is similar to hibernation but occurs during hot, dry periods. Some tortoises, like the African spurred tortoise, estivate by digging deep burrows to escape the scorching heat and conserve water. These clever survival strategies help turtles endure extreme environmental changes and emerge unscathed when conditions improve.

Regeneration and Healing

Turtles are incredibly resilient creatures, and they have an amazing ability to heal from injuries. Some species can even regenerate lost or damaged tissue, such as skin, shell, and bone.

When a turtle's shell is damaged, it can produce new layers of scutes to repair the injury. Over time, the new scutes will grow and harden, eventually restoring the shell to its original strength and appearance. This remarkable healing ability helps turtles bounce back from injuries that would be fatal to many other animals.

DIET & FEEDING

In this chapter, we'll explore the diverse and fascinating world of turtle diets and feeding habits. From plant-loving herbivores to skilled predators, turtles have a wide range of dietary preferences that help them thrive in various habitats.

HERBIVORES: THE PLANT EATERS

Many turtle species primarily feed on plant material, making them **herbivores**. Herbivorous turtles, like the green sea turtle and various species of tortoises, have broad, flat beaks that are perfect for crushing and grinding leaves, stems, and fruits.

Green sea turtles (left) are known for their love of seagrass, which makes up the majority of their diet. They play an essential role in maintaining healthy seagrass beds by grazing on the older, tougher blades, promoting new growth. On the other hand, tortoises like the African spurred tortoise enjoy a diverse diet of grasses, flowers, and succulents found in their arid habitats.

CARNIVORES: THE MEAT EATERS

Some turtle species are primarily **carnivores**, feeding on a variety of animals such as insects, fish, mollusks, and even other turtles. Carnivorous turtles, like the snapping turtle and the softshell turtle, have sharp, hooked beaks that help them capture and tear apart their prey.

Snapping turtles are skilled ambush predators, using their powerful jaws and lightning-fast reflexes to catch unsuspecting fish, frogs, and even small birds. Softshell turtles, with their long, flexible necks, can strike quickly and snatch up prey with surprising speed and accuracy.

OMNIVORES: THE BEST OF BOTH WORLDS

Many turtles are **omnivores**, which means they eat both plant and animal material. Omnivorous turtles, like the red-eared slider and the painted turtle, have a varied diet that includes aquatic plants, insects, crustaceans, and fish.

This dietary flexibility allows omnivorous turtles to take advantage of a wide range of food sources, making it easier for them to find a meal in their ever-changing environments. As they grow, the dietary preferences of some species may shift, with juveniles being more carnivorous and adults incorporating more plant material into their diets.

TURTLES IN DANGER

Sadly, turtles face many dangers in the wild. From pollution to climate change, it's getting harder and harder for turtles to survive. Fortunately, people like you want to help, and things can be done to protect their future.

HABITAT LOSS AND DESTRUCTION

One of the most significant threats to turtles is the loss and destruction of their habitats. As human populations expand, natural areas are being developed for agriculture, housing, and infrastructure, leaving turtles with fewer places to call home.

Sea turtles are particularly affected by coastal development, as their nesting beaches are often prime targets for construction projects like hotels and resorts. This can lead to the disturbance of nesting females and the destruction of nests.

Freshwater turtles suffer from the draining of wetlands, the construction of dams, and the pollution of rivers and lakes, which can degrade their habitats and impact their food sources.

POLLUTION AND PLASTIC WASTE

Pollution is a huge threat to turtles, both on land and in the water. Chemicals, heavy metals, and plastic waste can all have terrible effects on turtle populations.

Sea turtles are especially vulnerable to plastic pollution, as they often mistake floating plastic bags for jellyfish, one of their main food sources. Eating plastic can lead to blockages in their digestive systems, malnutrition, and even death.

Freshwater turtles can also be harmed by pollution, as toxins can pollute their habitats, affecting their health and ability to reproduce.

CLIMATE CHANGE

Climate change is also having a big impact on turtles, affecting their habitats, food sources, and even their reproduction. Rising sea levels, increasing temperatures, and more frequent extreme weather events all make it harder for turtles trying to survive.

For sea turtles, the temperature of the sand where they lay their eggs determines the sex of their offspring. With rising temperatures, there is a risk of producing too many female hatchlings, leading to a decline in population.

Freshwater turtles may also be affected by shifting climates, as changes in rainfall patterns and water levels can impact their habitats and the availability of food.

ILLEGAL TRADE AND EXPLOITATION

Many turtle species are at risk from illegal trade and exploitation, both for their meat, shells, and as pets. Poaching of eggs, hunting of adults, and the collection of wild turtles for the pet trade can all contribute to declining populations.

The critically endangered ploughshare tortoise from Madagascar is highly sought after in the illegal pet trade due to its beautiful golden shell, making it one of the rarest and most expensive tortoises in the world.

The hawksbill sea turtle is also hunted for its beautiful shell, which is used to make decorative items and jewelry, despite bans on products made from them.

CONSERVATION EFFORTS: SAVING OUR SHELLED FRIENDS

Fortunately, many organizations and individuals are working tirelessly to protect turtles and their habitats. Conservation efforts range from research and monitoring to habitat restoration and community outreach.

Groups like the **Sea Turtle Conservancy** and the **Turtle Survival Alliance** are dedicated to the protection of turtle species worldwide, through research, habitat protection, and education programs.

WHAT CAN <u>YOU</u> DO TO HELP?

From making small changes in your daily life to volunteering with local organizations, there are many opportunities to make a positive impact on the lives of turtles. Here are just a few ways you can help:

REDUCE, REUSE, AND RECYCLE

One of the easiest ways to help turtles is by reducing your waste and plastic consumption. By using reusable bags, bottles, and containers, you can help decrease the amount of plastic waste that ends up in our oceans and threatens marine life, including sea turtles.

Participate in beach cleanups or organize your own cleanup event with friends, family, or community members to help keep turtle habitats clean and safe.

KNOW ABOUT THE PRODUCTS YOU USE

Supporting sustainable and environmentally friendly products is another way to help protect turtle habitats and reduce the demand for products made from threatened species.

Avoid purchasing products made from turtle shells, such as jewelry or decorative items, as this can contribute to the illegal trade and exploitation of endangered species like the hawksbill sea turtle.

Choose sustainably sourced seafood to help protect marine ecosystems and reduce the impact of overfishing on turtle populations.

SUPPORT TURTLE CONSERVATION ORGANIZATIONS

There are many organizations dedicated to the conservation of turtles and their habitats. By donating to or volunteering with these groups, you can help support their important work.

Research and support local, national, or international turtle conservation organizations, such as the Sea Turtle Conservancy, the Turtle Survival Alliance, or the Marine Turtle Research Group.

Participate in volunteer opportunities like nest monitoring, beach cleanups, or habitat restoration projects to directly contribute to turtle conservation efforts.

Educating others about the importance of turtle conservation and the threats they face is a powerful way to help protect turtles.

Share your passion for turtles with friends, family, and your community by talking about their importance and the challenges they face.

Every little bit helps! By getting involved in conservation efforts, spreading awareness, and making eco-friendly choices, you'll play a vital role in ensuring the survival of turtles.

TURTLE
FUN FACTS

You've already learned so much about turtles, but there's still more to discover! Prepare to dive into a treasure trove of fascinating and delightful fun facts about turtles.

A Herman's tortoise.

The oldest known turtle fossil, called *Odontochelys semitestacea*, dates back around 220 million years.

• • •

Turtles are **ectothermic**, meaning their body temperature is regulated by their environment.

• • •

Some turtles can retract their heads into their shells for protection, while others, like sea turtles, have a fixed head and neck.

• • •

Turtles are found on every continent except Antarctica.

The temperature of a turtle's nest can determine the sex of the hatchlings: warmer temperatures produce more females, while cooler temperatures produce more males.

• • •

Turtles have been around since the time of the dinosaurs.

• • •

Sea turtles can travel thousands of miles during their migration to feed and reproduce.

• • •

A group of turtles is called a "**bale**."

A sea turtle.

A giant tortoise.

Some freshwater turtles can absorb oxygen through their skin and mouth lining, allowing them to stay underwater for extended periods.

• • •

Turtles have an excellent sense of smell, which helps them find food and mates.

• • •

Turtles can't hear very well, but they can detect vibrations in the water.

• • •

The leatherback sea turtle can dive deeper than 4,000 feet (1,219 m), making it the deepest diving reptile.

Box turtles are named for their hinged shell, which allows them to close up tightly like a box.

• • •

The largest sea turtle, the leatherback, can weigh over 1,500 pounds (680 kg) and measure up to 7 feet (2.1 m) in length.

• • •

The smallest turtle, the speckled padloper tortoise, is only about 3 inches (7.6 cm) long when fully grown.

• • •

Some turtles can live for more than 100 years, making them one of the longest-lived animals on Earth.

A box turtle.

African helmeted turtles are also known as marsh terrapins. They live both on land and in water.

Tortoises are land-dwelling turtles with high-domed shells and elephant-like feet.

. . .

Terrapins are turtles that spend time both in water and on land, often found in brackish water environments.

. . .

Many turtle species have specialized diets, like the hawksbill sea turtle, which feeds primarily on sponges.

. . .

The alligator snapping turtle has a worm-like appendage on its tongue to lure fish into its mouth.

Hawksbill turtles.

The fastest turtle on land is the common snapping turtle, which can reach speeds of 3 miles (4.8 km) per hour.

• • •

The matamata turtle has a flattened, leaf-like head to help it blend into its surroundings and ambush prey.

• • •

Turtles have a third eyelid called the nictitating membrane, which helps protect their eyes when they're underwater.

The ploughshare tortoise (below) has a distinctive gular scute (front part of the lower shell) that's shaped like a plow, used for flipping rival males during fights.

• • •

Turtles have been featured on many countries' postage stamps and coins, often as symbols of environmental conservation.

Some turtle species can hibernate during cold months by burying themselves in mud or sand.

• • •

The Indian flapshell turtle has flexible flaps on its shell that allow it to tightly seal itself inside when threatened.

• • •

Turtles have been kept as pets for thousands of years, with evidence of ancient Egyptians and Romans keeping them in captivity.

• • •

The painted turtle is the most widespread native turtle species in North America.

The pig-nosed turtle is the only freshwater turtle with flippers, similar to those of sea turtles.

. . .

Turtles have a good sense of direction and are known to return to the same nesting sites year after year.

. . .

The spiny softshell turtle has a leathery, flexible shell covered in small spines, giving it a unique appearance.

. . .

Turtles have been featured in folklore and legends worldwide, often symbolizing wisdom, longevity, and stability.

The snake-necked turtle has a long, snake-like neck that it uses to strike at prey with lightning speed.

The diamondback terrapin is the only turtle species in the United States that lives in brackish water habitats like estuaries and salt marshes.

· · ·

The pancake tortoise has a flat, flexible shell that allows it to squeeze into rock crevices to escape predators.

· · ·

The big-headed turtle has a disproportionately large head that it can't retract into its shell.

· · ·

The Mary River turtle, native to Australia, has algae growing on its head, giving it a green, "punk rock" appearance.

The Galapagos giant tortoise is the largest living species of tortoise, with some individuals weighing more than 900 pounds (408 kg).

• • •

The loggerhead sea turtle is named for its large, powerful head, which helps it crush the shells of its prey.

• • •

The Chinese softshell turtle can excrete urea through its mouth, allowing it to stay submerged in water for longer periods.

• • •

Turtles have a lower shell called the plastron and an upper shell called the carapace, which are fused to their spine and ribcage.

The Asian forest tortoise,
also known as the
Mountain tortoise, is the
largest tortoise in Asia.
It can reach weights of
around 55 lb (25 kg)!

The olive ridley sea turtle is known for its mass nesting events called "arribadas," during which thousands of females come ashore to lay their eggs.

. . .

The yellow-blotched map turtle is named for the intricate, map-like patterns on its shell.

. . .

The Arrau turtle is the largest side-necked turtle, with a shell length of up to 3.3 feet (1 m).

. . .

The Blanding's turtle is known for its bright yellow chin and throat, as well as its long neck.

Were you paying attention?! Test your new turtle knowledge in our quiz!

1   What are the three main groups of turtles?

2   Name the two parts of a turtle's shell.

3   Which turtle species has a worm-like appendage on its tongue to lure fish?

4   How does the temperature of a turtle's nest affect the sex of the hatchlings?

5   What is the largest species of sea turtle?

6   What is the smallest turtle species?

7   Which turtle species has a shell covered in small spines?

8   What does the term "ectothermic" mean?

16 Which turtle species has a disproportionately large head that it can't retract into its shell?

17 What is the purpose of a turtle's nictitating membrane?

18 Which turtle species is named for the map-like patterns on its shell?

19 What is the largest living species of tortoise?

20 Name one conservation organization dedicated to the protection of turtles.

21 How can reducing plastic waste help turtles?

ANSWERS

1. Sea turtles, freshwater turtles and tortoises.
2. Carapace (upper shell) and plastron (lower shell)
3. Alligator snapping turtle
4. Warmer temperatures produce more females, while cooler temperatures produce more males.
5. Leatherback sea turtle
6. Speckled padloper tortoise
7. Spiny softshell turtle
8. Ectothermic means that an animal's body temperature is regulated by its environment.
9. Common snapping turtle
10. Sponges
11. Through their skin or mouth lining

12. Green sea turtle
13. Bale
14. Illegal wildlife trade and habitat loss
15. Olive ridley sea turtle
16. Big-headed turtle
17. To protect their eyes when they're underwater
18. Yellow-blotched map turtle
19. Galapagos giant tortoise
20. Sea Turtle Conservancy, Turtle Survival Alliance, or Marine Turtle Research Group (any one of these is correct)
21. Reducing plastic waste helps prevent plastic pollution in the oceans, which can harm marine life, including sea turtles.

Can you find all the words below in the word search puzzle on the right?

AQUATIC	REPTILE	SHELL
TORTOISE	OMNIVORE	FLIPPER
HATCHLING	ECOSYSTEM	SNAPPING

```
S D S X S R E P T I L E
N A B J Q H S D F H J K
A W Q Q H G E C V F N U
P E U U Q J H L C L R T
P D Y H A T C H L I N G
I V M J H T X D S P C G
N T O R T O I S E P J F
G Y T R Z D F C V E U D
E C O S Y S T E M R R A
N Q G R D S W F Z X W O
B O M N I V O R E C D U
X H G F S R G J K D F Y
```

SOLUTION

S				S	R	E	P	T	I	L	E
N	A				H						
A		Q			E			F			
P			U			L		L			
P			H	A	T	C	H	L	I	N	G
I				T				P			
N	T	O	R	T	O	I	S	E	P		
G					C		E				
E	C	O	S	Y	S	T	E	M	R		
	O	M	N	I	V	O	R	E			

SOURCES

Auffenberg, W. (1977). The Biology and Conservation of the Gopher Tortoise. In Proceedings: Rare and Endangered Wildlife Symposium.

Buhlmann, K. A., Tuberville, T. D., & Gibbons, J. W. (2008). Turtles of the Southeast. University of Georgia Press.

Dodd, C. K. (2001). North American Box Turtles: A Natural History. University of Oklahoma Press.

Ernst, C. H., & Lovich, J. E. (2009). Turtles of the United States and Canada. Johns Hopkins University Press.

Frazier, J. G. (2005). Marine turtles: The role of culture and myth in shaping today's conservation efforts. In Marine Turtle Newsletter.

Hershler, R., & Mikkelsen, P. M. (2004). Marine Turtles in the Indo-Pacific: History, Distribution, and Biology. In Marine Turtles in the Indo-Pacific: Research, Management, and Conservation.

Highfield, A. C. (1996). Practical Encyclopedia of Keeping and Breeding Tortoises and Freshwater Turtles. Carapace Press.

Lutz, P. L., & Musick, J. A. (Eds.). (1997). The Biology of Sea Turtles. CRC Press.

National Geographic. (2021). Turtle Facts. Retrieved from https://www.nationalgeographic.com/animals/reptiles/group/turtles/

Orenstein, R. I. (2001). Turtles, Tortoises & Terrapins: Survivors in Armor. Firefly Books.

Pritchard, P. C. H. (1979). Encyclopedia of Turtles. T.F.H. Publications.

Sea Turtle Conservancy. (2021). Information About Sea Turtles. Retrieved from https://conserveturtles.org/information-sea-turtles/

Spotila, J. R. (2004). Sea Turtles: A Complete Guide to their Biology, Behavior, and Conservation. Johns Hopkins University Press.

Turtle Survival Alliance. (2021). Species Profiles. Retrieved from https://turtlesurvival.org/species-profiles/

Wyneken, J., Lohmann, K. J., & Musick, J. A. (Eds.). (2013). The Biology of Sea Turtles, Volume III. CRC Press.

You're Turtley Awesome!

As our journey through the world of turtles comes to an end, we hope you've enjoyed learning about these fascinating reptiles as much as we enjoyed sharing their story with you!

Your feedback means a lot to us, so we kindly ask you to leave a review on the platform where you purchased the book.

Your thoughts and experiences will help other readers discover the wonderful world of turtles.

Thank you for your support!

ALSO BY JENNY KELLETT

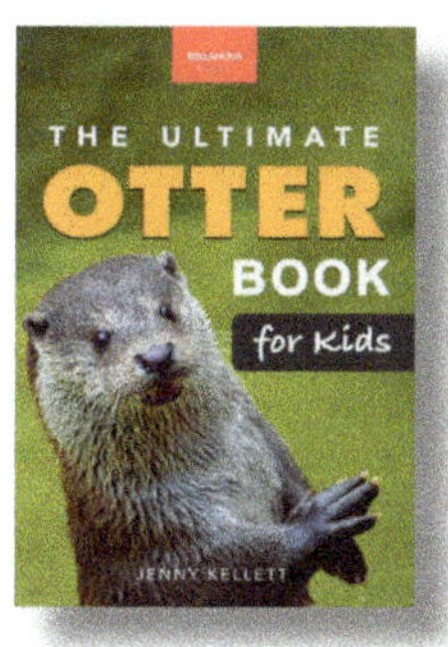

... and more!

Available at

www.bellanovabooks.com

and all major online bookstores.

9 7 8 6 1 9 2 6 4 1 6 9 6